DINOSAUR DIG

Dinosaurs in Action

Unearth the secrets behind dinosaur fossils

QEB Publishing

Rupert Matthews

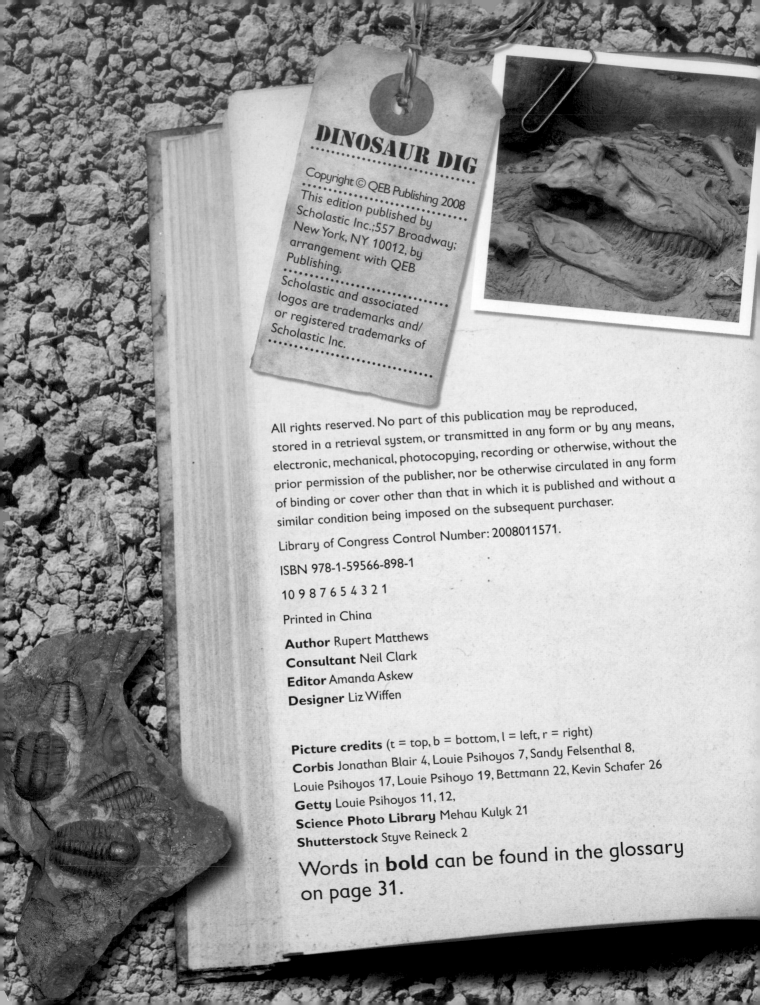

Library of Congress Control Number: 2008011571.

ISBN 978-1-59566-898-1

10 9 8 7 6 5 4 3 2 1

Printed in China

Author Rupert Matthews
Consultant Neil Clark
Editor Amanda Askew
Designer Liz Wiffen

Picture credits (t = top, b = bottom, l = left, r = right)
Corbis Jonathan Blair 4, Louie Psihoyos 7, Sandy Felsenthal 8, Louie Psihoyos 17, Louie Psihoyo 19, Bettmann 22, Kevin Schafer 26
Getty Louie Psihoyos 11, 12,
Science Photo Library Mehau Kulyk 21
Shutterstock Styve Reineck 2

Words in **bold** can be found in the glossary on page 31.

CONTENTS

DINO GUIDE

For every dinosaur in this book and many more, learn how to pronounce their name, find out their length and weight, and discover what they ate.

DINOSAUR DIG

Dinosaurs **were a group of** reptiles **that lived on Earth millions of years ago.**

There were many different types of dinosaur. Some dinosaurs had feathers or were brightly colored. The legs of modern reptiles, such as lizards, stick out sideways. Dinosaurs, however, had legs that were tucked under their body.

⬤ *A **paleontologist** (pay-lee-on-toll-oh-jist) excavates, or digs up, the **skull** and **skeleton** of Albertosaurus (al-bert-oh-saw-rus), a hunting dinosaur from the Cretaceous Period.*

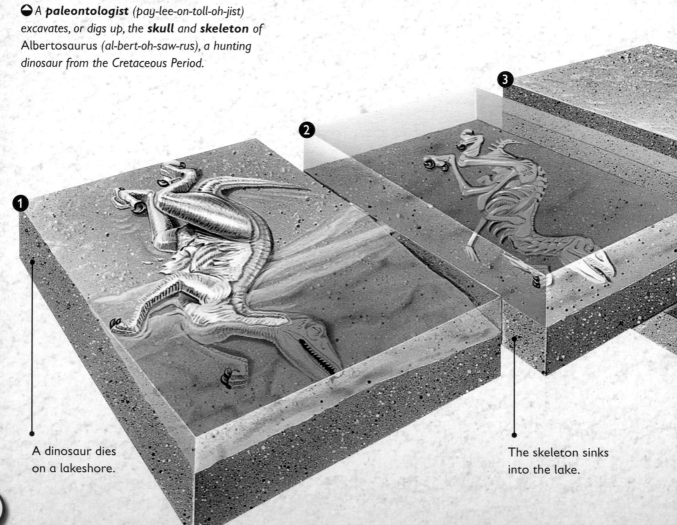

1 A dinosaur dies on a lakeshore.

3 The skeleton sinks into the lake.

Some dinosaurs could run quickly, or leap and jump. Others walked slowly with heavy steps. Some dinosaurs had sharp teeth and claws to attack their prey. A few dinosaurs had growths on their head, back, or sides. All dinosaurs were alert, active reptiles.

How big were dinosaurs?

Every dinosaur is compared to an average adult, about 5 ft. 5 in. (1.68 m) in height, to show just how big they really were.

When a plant or animal dies, it usually rots away completely. However, in special conditions, parts of it can become fossilized.

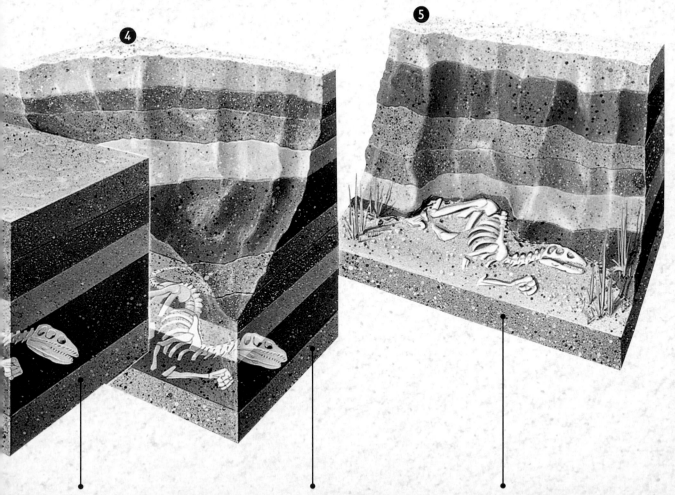

Layers of mud settle over the skeleton. The mud and bones gradually turn into stone.

The rock wears away, or **erodes.**

As more rock erodes, the skeleton is revealed.

DINOSAUR RUNNERS

Dinosaurs could run well. This skill was important for chasing prey and escaping from danger.

As their legs grew straight down from the hips, dinosaurs only needed to move their legs in order to walk or run. Other reptiles need to swing their body from side to side because their legs grow out from the sides. Therefore, dinosaurs could move fast while using less energy.

Coelophysis (see-low-fye-sis) was an early hunting dinosaur. It ran on its back legs. *Coelophysis* was fast and agile enough to grab a smaller animal. It was also able to flee quickly from danger.

DINOSAUR DIG
Coelophysis

WHERE: New Mexico, North America

PERIOD: 225 million years ago in the late Triassic

DIG SITE

WOW!

There are two dinosaur groups. The ornithischians had hips like modern birds, and the saurischians had hips like modern lizards.

◐ *Dinosaurs and other animals flee as fire sweeps across the Triassic landscape of North America. Events like this are recorded in the fossil record—a list of all the fossils ever discovered.*

◑ A **fossil** skeleton of Coelophysis. The remains of its last meal have been preserved inside its stomach.

Coelophysis

10 ft. (3 m) in length

STRIPPING LEAVES

Sauropod **dinosaurs were the biggest dinosaurs of all, but they had the smallest mouths.**

The leaves and shoots that sauropods ate did not give much energy. As they were so big, sauropods ate huge amounts of food every day to survive.

It is thought that sauropods did not chew their food at all. They bit off a mouthful of leaves and swallowed them whole. Sauropods swallowed stones that were moved around by the stomach muscles to help digest the leaves and twigs.

DINOSAUR DIG
Brachiosaurus

WHERE: Colorado, North America

PERIOD: 150 million years ago in the late Jurassic

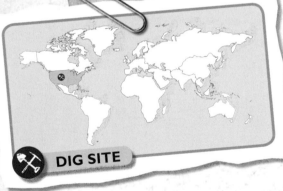

DIG SITE

◑ *A fossilized skull of Brachiosaurus (brack-ee-oh-saw-rus). The large openings in the skull were for the eyes and nostrils. The huge nostrils may have contained veins carrying blood that was cooled by the air as it breathed in.*

● *Brachiosaurus takes a mouthful of leaves from a tree. Its long neck allowed Brachiosaurus to eat food that other dinosaurs could not reach.*

Brachiosaurus

80 ft. (24.4 m) in length

9

Animals rely on their sense of hearing, especially if they live in dense forests where it is difficult to see for more than a few feet (meters).

Hunters listen for prey, and plant eaters listen for nearby hunters. Dinosaur ears were fairly simple. It is thought that they did not have ear flaps. There was probably just a simple hole leading to the inner ear.

DINOSAUR DIG
Allosaurus

WHERE: Wyoming, North America

PERIOD: 150 million years ago in the late Jurassic

DIG SITE

WOW!

If a dinosaur put its jaws on the ground, it could "hear" vibrations made by the footsteps of nearby animals.

◐ Allosaurus (al-oh-saw-rus) stops to listen to a sound—it may be prey nearby. Hearing is a key sense for hunting animals and may make the difference between a successful hunt and hunger.

◑ A fossilized skeleton of Allosaurus. The large, powerful head and strong claws on the front limbs show it was an active hunter.

Allosaurus was a large hunter that preyed on sauropods, preferring to attack old or weak individuals as they would have been easier to kill.

Allosaurus

40 ft. (12.2 m) in length

Microraptor (my-krow-rap-tor), meaning "tiny hunter," was named by the scientist who found it because it looked like a small hunting dinosaur.

Then it was noticed that the dinosaur had feathers growing from its arms, legs, and tail. The feathers were long and strong, like those of a modern bird. However, its muscles were not strong enough for it to fly.

DINOSAUR DIG
Microraptor

WHERE: Liaoning, China, Asia

PERIOD: 130 million years ago in the early Cretaceous

DIG SITE

◐ A *Microraptor* fossil preserved in rock. The feathers can be clearly seen around the bones. Delicate features, such as feathers, are rarely preserved.

It is now thought that *Microraptor* used its feathers to glide for short distances. It may have lived in forests, where it climbed trees to look for insects to feed on. The tail was probably used to control steering in the air.

⬤ *Microraptor probably glided from one tree to the next to escape from danger or to pounce on food.*

Microraptor

2 ft. (0.6 m) in length

WOW!

In 1999, a man glued the front end of a *Microraptor* fossil to the back end of a different dinosaur fossil. He then pretended that he had found a new type of dinosaur, but the truth was soon revealed.

HIBERNATION

Although the Earth was warmer and wetter during the time of the dinosaurs, there were areas with cooler weather.

Australia and New Zealand lay close to the South Pole about 110 million years ago. During winter, the sun did not shine for weeks on end. The weather was very cold and no plants would grow.

Some of the larger dinosaurs may have walked to warmer areas in winter, but smaller dinosaurs could not escape. Instead, they hibernated.

When an animal hibernates, it goes into a very deep sleep. The heart rate and breathing slow down, the body temperature drops, and all bodily functions become slower. During this time, the creature survives on fat stored in its body.

DINOSAUR DIG
Leaellynasaura

Timimus

WHERE: Southern Australia

PERIOD: 106 million years ago in the early Cretaceous

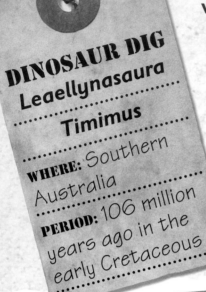

DIG SITE

WOW!

Scientists did not know that dinosaurs lived in cold parts of the world until the fossil of *Leaellynasaura* was found in Australia in the late 1900s.

A scene from Australia about 106 million years ago. The larger dinosaur Timimus (tim-ee-mus) hibernates under a log while a group of smaller Leaellynasaura (lee-ell-in-ah-saw-rah) look up at the Southern Lights.

Leaellynasaura

6.5 ft. (2 m) in length

Timimus

11 ft. (3.4 m) in length

INTO THE FUTURE

Paleontologists believe that birds come from small hunting dinosaurs. They both have feathers, walk on their back legs, and have hollow limb bones.

Some scientists think that the two groups are so similar that they should belong to a single group. They believe that dinosaurs did not become **extinct**, they just became birds instead.

DINOSAUR DIG
Archaeopteryx

WHERE: Southern Germany, Europe

PERIOD: 155 million years ago in the late Jurassic

DIG SITE

Other scientists point out the differences between the groups. Dinosaurs had teeth, birds do not. Birds can fly, most dinosaurs could not. These scientists think that dinosaurs and birds should continue to be seen as different groups of animals.

WOW!

Some scientists think that birds come from a particular family of dinosaurs called the tetanurans, which later **evolved** into the tyrannosaurs.

◑ This fossilized Archaeopteryx (ark-ee-op-tur-iks) shows the feathers and how they are arranged to form two wings. When this fossil was found, it showed a link between dinosaurs and birds.

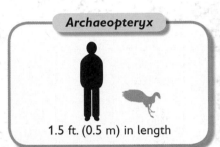

Archaeopteryx

1.5 ft. (0.5 m) in length

◑ Archaeopteryx perches on a tree branch. Scientists think that Archaeopteryx was a good flyer, but only over short distances.

The sense of smell is important to most animals. Plant eaters can smell a hunter from some distance away and may flee before it becomes a danger.

Hunters use scent to track down prey. Also, if the wind is blowing away from the hunter, their victim will not be able to smell them approaching.

The parts of the nose that are used to smell are never fossilized. Therefore, scientists cannot be certain how well dinosaurs could smell. However, some species have long, twisted nostrils that contained scent receptors, so these dinosaurs could probably smell better than others.

DINOSAUR DIG
Velociraptor
WHERE: Mongolia, Asia
WHEN: 75 million years ago in the late Cretaceous

DIG SITE

◑ *A **pack** of Velociraptors (vel-oss-ee-rap-tor) moves through a Cretaceous forest. There is some evidence that these dinosaurs hunted as a group, working together to hunt and kill prey.*

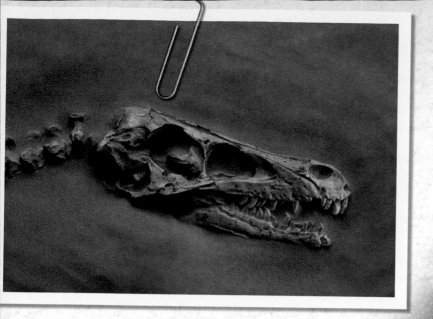

◗ *This fossilized skull of a Velociraptor shows that this dinosaur had around 80 sharp, curved teeth set in long narrow jaws. This was ideal for eating meat once prey had been killed.*

Velociraptor

6.5 ft. (2 m) in length

19

A TASTY SNACK

It is usually thought that larger hunters preyed on large plant eaters.

However, even the biggest hunter would have snapped up a much smaller animal if it got the chance. A baby dinosaur or other small creature would have been killed instantly by one bite of the giant jaws.

Scientists think that the big hunters had such strong chemicals in their stomach that they may have been able to digest the bones. Others think that the bones were regurgitated once the meat had been digested.

DINOSAUR DIG
Tarbosaurus

WHERE: Mongolia, Asia

WHEN: 70 million years ago in the late Cretaceous

DIG SITE

WOW!

Tarbosaurus lived in Asia and *Tyrannosaurus* (tie-rann-oh-saw-rus) rex in America, but they were very similar. Some scientists believe they were the same animal.

◗ *The hunter Tarbosaurus (tar-bow-saw-rus) prepares to snap up a young hadrosaur. Its long, stabbing teeth and powerful jaws would kill such a small animal with a single bite.*

Tarbosaurus was a tyrannosaur that grew to more than 40 ft. (12.2 m) in length. Like other tyrannosaurs, it had very powerful jaws, but tiny front arms. Some scientists think that *Tarbosaurus* could not tackle large dinosaurs, so it fed on smaller animals or **carrion**.

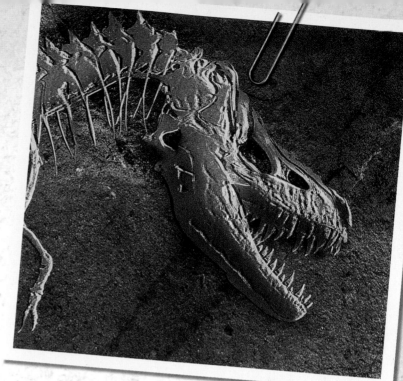

⬤ *The fossilized head and neck of Tarbosaurus show that this dinosaur had a deep snout and jaws attached to very powerful muscles. Its bite was probably strong enough to crush bones.*

Tarbosaurus

40 ft. (12.2 m) in length

A GAME OF BLUFF

When they meet a dangerous hunter or rival, many animals will try to make themselves look bigger and stronger than they really are. They hope that this will frighten off the other animal.

Many scientists think that **ceratopian** dinosaurs used their **neck frill** as a **bluffing** weapon. The frill looked large and impressive. The animal would lift up its frill so that it looked as big as possible, then move it from side to side. It was actually made of a thin layer of bone and skin. The frill may also have been used to attract females for mating.

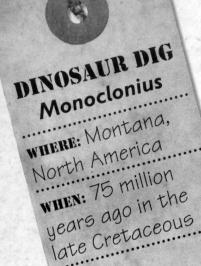

DINOSAUR DIG
Monoclonius

WHERE: Montana, North America

WHEN: 75 million years ago in the late Cretaceous

DIG SITE

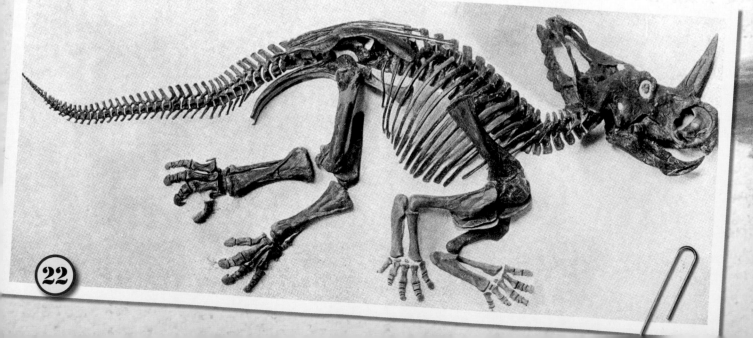

⬤ *A rare complete skeleton of Monoclonius (mon-oh-clone-ee-us). Usually only part of the skeleton is found. A skeleton such as this allows scientists to see the complete animal.*

Monoclonius

16.5 ft. (5 m) in length

🔘 *Monoclonius lowers its head and stamps on the ground with its front feet to prepare for a fight. Combats may have been between rivals of the same species, or against hunters.*

ALARM!

Plant eaters that live in herds or flocks usually have a way of warning others if danger threatens.

Some animals will call loudly or stamp their feet on the ground to make a noise. Others have brightly colored parts of their body that they will reveal suddenly, flashing a patch of color on and off.

DINOSAUR DIG

Anserimimus
....
Oviraptor
....
Protoceratops
....
Tarbosaurus
....
WHERE: Mongolia, Asia
....
WHEN: 75 million years ago in the late Cretaceous
....

DIG SITE

Protoceratops

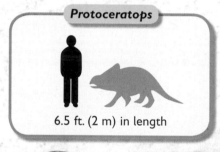

6.5 ft. (2 m) in length

A pair of Protoceratops *(pro-toe-ser-ah-tops) guard their nest.*

Oviraptor

6.5 ft. (2 m) in length

Some dinosaurs had brightly colored feathers growing from their tail. These may have been used as an alarm signal. The dinosaur would show the back of the fan as it fled from danger. Other dinosaurs would follow because they knew that they would also be running away from the hunting dinosaur.

◐ *A tyrannosaur chases* Anserimimus *(ann-sair-ee-me-mus) and* Oviraptor *(oh-vee-rap-tor).*

Anserimimus

10 ft. (3 m) in length

Tarbosaurus

40 ft. (12.2 m) in length

FINAL BATTLE

As conditions changed, new types of dinosaur gradually evolved and older types died out.

Sauropods became much rarer and stegosaurs died out completely. They were replaced by ceratopians and hadrosaurs.

Suddenly, about 65 million years ago, all the dinosaurs became extinct. Many other types of animal died out at the same time.

Scientists are not certain what caused this mass extinction. Some think that a meteorite hit the Earth, wiping out huge numbers of animals. Others think that a sudden change in climate caused the deaths.

DINOSAUR DIG

Triceratops ....

Tyrannosaurus ....

WHERE: Colorado, North America ....

WHEN: 65 million years ago in the late Cretaceous ....

DIG SITE

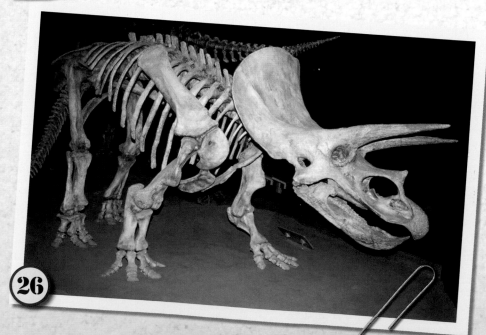

◖ *This skeleton of* Triceratops *(try-ser-ah-tops) shows both the long, sharp horns and the large neck frill. It was a sturdy, powerful animal.*

◆ Triceratops *prepares to face* Tyrannosaurus *(tie-rann-oh-saw-rus) rex in battle.* Tyrannosaurus rex *would have tried to avoid the sharp horns of its prey.*

WOW!

When the first dinosaur fossils were found, people thought they were the bones of giant men.

Tyrannosaurus

40 ft. (12.2 m) in length

Triceratops

30 ft. (9.1 m) in length

DINO GUIDE

Coelophysis (p6)

PRONUNCIATION
see-low-fye-sis
LENGTH 10 ft. (3 m)
WEIGHT 75–80 lbs. (28–30 kg)
DIET Small animals

Efraasia

PRONUNCIATION
ef-rah-see-ah
LENGTH 23 ft. (7 m)
WEIGHT 1,300 lbs. (492 kg)
DIET Plants

Eoraptor
PRONUNCIATION
ee-oh-rap-tor
LENGTH 3 ft. (1 m)
WEIGHT 7–30 lbs. (2.6–11 kg)
DIET Small animals

Herrerasaurus
PRONUNCIATION
he-ray-ra-saw-rus
LENGTH 10 ft. (3 m)
WEIGHT 450 lbs. (170 kg)
DIET Animals

Pisanosaurus

PRONUNCIATION
peez-an-oh-saw-rus
LENGTH 3 ft. (1 m)
WEIGHT 6.5 lbs. (2.5 kg)
DIET Plants

Plateosaurus

PRONUNCIATION
plat-ee-oh-saw-rus
LENGTH 26 ft. (8 m)
WEIGHT 1 ton (0.9 tonne)
DIET Plants

Procompsognathus
PRONUNCIATION
pro-comp-sog-nay-thus
LENGTH 4 ft. (1.2 m)
WEIGHT 4.5–6.5 lbs. (1.7–2.5 kg)
DIET Small animals

Riojasaurus
PRONUNCIATION
ree-oh-ha-saw-rus
LENGTH 33 ft. (10 m)
WEIGHT 1 ton (0.9 tonne)
DIET Plants

Saltopus
PRONUNCIATION
sall-toe-puss
LENGTH Less than 3 ft. (1 m)
WEIGHT 2–4.5 lbs. (0.7–1.7 kg)
DIET Small animals

Staurikosaurus

PRONUNCIATION
store-ick-oh-saw-rus
LENGTH 6.5 ft. (2 m)
WEIGHT 65 lbs. (24.5 kg)
DIET Small animals

JURASSIC PERIOD
206 TO 145
MILLION YEARS AGO

Allosaurus (p10)
PRONUNCIATION
al-oh-saw-rus
LENGTH 40 ft. (12.2 m)
WEIGHT 1.5–2 tons (1.4–1.8 tonnes)
DIET Animals

Apatosaurus
PRONUNCIATION
ap-at-oh-saw-rus
LENGTH 80 ft. (24.4 m)
WEIGHT 25–35 tons (23–32 tonnes)
DIET Plants

Archaeopteryx (p16)
PRONUNCIATION
ark-ee-op-tur-iks
LENGTH 1.5 ft. (0.5 m)
WEIGHT 1 lb. (0.4 kg)
DIET Animals

Brachiosaurus (p8)
PRONUNCIATION
brack-ee-oh-saw-rus
LENGTH 80 ft. (24.4 m)
WEIGHT 50 tons (45 tonnes)
DIET Plants

Camptosaurus
PRONUNCIATION
kamp-toe-saw-rus
LENGTH 20 ft. (6.1 m)
WEIGHT 1–2 tons (0.9–1.8 tonnes)
DIET Plants

Cetiosaurus
PRONUNCIATION
set-ee-oh-saw-rus
LENGTH 60 ft. (18.3 m)
WEIGHT 15–20 tons (14–18 tonnes)
DIET Plants

Compsognathus
PRONUNCIATION
comp-sog-nay-thus
LENGTH 3–5 ft. (1–1.5 m)
WEIGHT 6.5 lbs. (2.5 kg)
DIET Small animals

Dicraeosaurus
PRONUNCIATION
die-kree-oh-saw-rus
LENGTH 43–65 ft. (13–20 m)
WEIGHT 10 tons (9 tonnes)
DIET Plants

Kentrosaurus
PRONUNCIATION
ken-troe-saw-rus
LENGTH 16.5 ft. (5 m)
WEIGHT 2 tons (1.8 tonnes)
DIET Plants

Megalosaurus
PRONUNCIATION
meg-ah-low-saw-rus
LENGTH 30 ft. (9 m)
WEIGHT 1 ton (0.9 tonne)
DIET Plants

CRETACEOUS PERIOD
145 TO 65 MILLION YEARS AGO

Albertosaurus (p4)
PRONUNCIATION
al-bert-oh-saw-rus
LENGTH 30 ft. (9 m)
WEIGHT 2.5 tons (2.3 tonnes)
DIET Animals

Oviraptor (p24)
PRONUNCIATION
oh-vee-rap-tor
LENGTH 6.5 ft. (2 m)
WEIGHT 65 lbs. (24.5 kg)
DIET Small animals and plants

Anserimimus (p24)
PRONUNCIATION
ann-sair-ee-me-mus
LENGTH 10 ft. (3 m)
WEIGHT 650 lbs. (246 kg)
DIET Small animals

Protoceratops (p24)
PRONUNCIATION
pro-toe-ser-ah-tops
LENGTH 6.5 ft. (2 m)
WEIGHT 330–550 lbs. (125–208 kg)
DIET Plants

Centrosaurus (p23)
PRONUNCIATION
sen-tro-saw-rus
LENGTH 20 ft. (6.1 m)
WEIGHT 3 tons (2.7 tonnes)
DIET Plants

Tarbosaurus (p20 and 24)
PRONUNCIATION
tar-bow-saw-rus
LENGTH 40 ft. (12.2 m)
WEIGHT 4 tons (3.6 tonnes)
DIET Large animals

Leaellynasaura (p14)
PRONUNCIATION
lee-ell-in-ah-saw-rah
LENGTH 6.5 ft. (2 m)
WEIGHT 22 lbs. (8.3 kg)
DIET Plants

Timimus (p14)
PRONUNCIATION
tim-ee-mus
LENGTH 11 ft. (3.4 m)
WEIGHT 650 lbs. (246 kg)
DIET Unknown

Microraptor (p12)
PRONUNCIATION
my-krow-rap-tor
LENGTH 2 ft. (0.6 m)
WEIGHT 2 lbs. (0.8 kg)
DIET Small animals

Triceratops (p26)
PRONUNCIATION
try-ser-ah-tops
LENGTH 30 ft. (9 m)
WEIGHT 5–8 tons (4.5–7.3 tonnes)
DIET Plants

Monoclonius (p22)
PRONUNCIATION
mon-oh-clone-ee-us
LENGTH 16.5 ft. (5 m)
WEIGHT 2–3 tons (1.8–2.7 tonnes)
DIET Plants

Tyrannosaurus rex (p20, 27)

PRONUNCIATION
tie-rann-oh-saw-rus
LENGTH 40 ft. (12.2 m)
WEIGHT 6 tons (5.4 tonnes)
DIET Large animals

Velociraptor (p18)

PRONUNCIATION
vel-oss-ee-rap-tor
LENGTH 6.5 ft. (2 m)
WEIGHT 45–65 lbs. (17–25 kg)
DIET Small animals

GLOSSARY

Bluff To deceive someone by pretending to be someone else.

Carrion Meat from a dead animal that the hunter has not killed itself.

Ceratopian A group of dinosaurs that had a neck frill and teeth designed for slicing. Most ceratopians also had horns on their head.

Cretaceous The third period of time in the age of the dinosaurs. The Cretaceous began about 145 million years ago and ended about 65 million years ago.

Dinosaur A type of reptile that lived millions of years ago. All dinosaurs are now extinct.

Erode To wear away.

Extinct Not existing any more. An animal is extinct when they have all died out.

Evolve To develop gradually over a long period of time.

Fossil Any part of a plant or animal that has been preserved in rock. Also traces of plants or animals, such as footprints.

Jurassic The second period of time in the age of the dinosaurs. The Jurassic

began about 206 million years ago and ended about 145 million years ago.

Neck frill A thin plate of bone and skin growing from the back of an animal's skull.

Pack A group of hunting animals.

Paleontologist A scientist who studies ancient forms of life, including dinosaurs.

Regurgitate To bring swallowed food up from the stomach into the mouth.

Reptile A cold-blooded animal, such as a lizard. Dinosaurs were reptiles, too.

Sauropod A type of dinosaur that had a long neck and tail. Sauropods included the largest of all dinosaurs.

Skeleton The bones in an animal's body.

Skull The bones of the head of an animal. The skull does not include the jaw, but many skulls have jaws attached.

Triassic The first period of time in the age of the dinosaurs. The Triassic began about 248 million years ago and ended about 208 million years ago.

INDEX